MW01004569

How Toys Float

Helen Whittaker

This edition first published in 2012 in the United States of America by Smart Apple Media.
All rights reserved. No part of this book may be reproduced in any form or by any means without written permission from the publisher.

Smart Apple Media
P.O. Box 3263
Mankato, MN, 56002

First published in 2011 by
MACMILLAN EDUCATION AUSTRALIA PTY LTD
15–19 Claremont Street, South Yarra 3141

Visit our website at www.macmillan.com.au or go directly to www.macmillanlibrary.com.au

Associated companies and representatives throughout the world.

Copyright © Macmillan Publishers Australia 2011

Library of Congress Cataloging-in-Publication Data has been applied for.

Publisher: Carmel Heron
Commissioning Editor: Niki Horin
Managing Editor: Vanessa Lanaway
Editors: Emma de Smit and Tim Clarke
Proofreader: Helena Newton
Designer: Kerri Wilson
Page layout: Romy Pearse
Photo researcher: Wendy Duncan (management: Debbie Gallagher)
Illustrator: Ned Culic (Colourist: Natalie Stuart)
Production Controller: Vanessa Johnson

Manufactured in China by Macmillan Production (Asia) Ltd.
Kwun Tong, Kowloon, Hong Kong
Supplier Code: CP March 2011

Acknowledgements
The publisher would like to thank Heidi Ruhnau, Head of Science at Oxley College, Victoria, for her assistance in reviewing manuscripts.

The author and publisher are grateful to the following for permission to reproduce copyright material:

Front cover photograph: Boy with toy sailboat © Corbis/Blend Images/ColorBlind Images.

Photographs courtesy of: Corbis/Blend Images/ColorBlind Images, 1, 5 (top), /Eyetrigger Pty Ltd, 4 (bottom left), /Radius Images, 8 (top), 10; Getty Images/National Geographic/Tim Laman, 5 (bottom), /Skip Brown, 9 (centre), 16; iStockphoto/NoDerog, 6; MEA Images/Image Source, 4 (bottom centre); photolibrary/Alamy/Aurora Photos, 4 (bottom right), /Alamy/Chuck Franklin, 9 (bottom), 18, /Alamy/Image Quest Marine/James D. Watt, 8 (bottom), 12, /Big Cheese, 20, /demotix, 9 (top), 14; Pixmac/Yuri Arcurs , 4 (top left); Shutterstock/cassiede alain, 4 (top right), /Michael William, 4 (top centre).

While every care has been taken to trace and acknowledge copyright, the publisher tenders their apologies for any accidental infringement where copyright has proved untraceable. They would be pleased to come to a suitable arrangement with the rightful owner in each case.

Contents

When a word is printed in **bold**, you can look up its meaning in the Glossary on page 31.

Toys and Forces

Forces make toys work. Forces make toys start moving, change direction, speed up, slow down, and stop moving. Forces also change the shape of some toys.

Bouncing toys

Floating toys

Flying toys

Rolling toys

Sliding toys

Spinning toys

None of these toys would work without forces.

What Is a Force?

A force is a push or a pull. When you push something, it moves away from you. When you pull something, it moves towards you.

When this boy applies a pushing force to the toy sailboat, it moves away from him.

When this boy applies a pulling force to the kayak, it moves towards him.

How Does a Floating Toy Work?

A floating toy can float on water because water pushes up against it. The water's pushing force stops the toy from **sinking**. Many toys that float on water are very light.

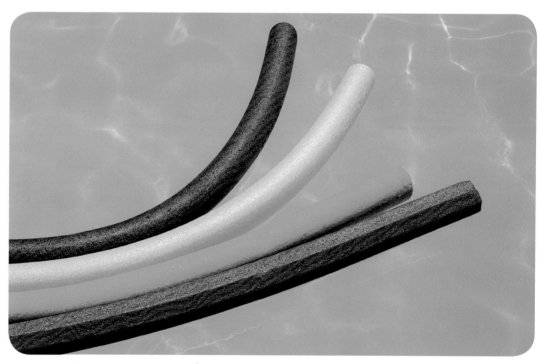

These pool noodles are very light and float because the water pushes them up.

Some heavier floating toys are shaped so that lots of water pushes up against them. The pushing force stops them sinking.

This model ship floats because its shape lets lots of water push up against it.

pushing force

How Do Forces Make Floating Toys Work?

Different forces make floating toys work. Pushes and pulls make the toys work in different ways. Forces can make floating toys work in these ways.

Forces can make floating toys start moving.

Forces can make floating toys change direction.

Forces can make floating toys speed up.

Forces can make floating toys slow down.

Forces can make floating toys stop moving.

What Makes a Floating Toy Start Moving?

When forces act on a floating toy, they can make it start moving. One force that can make a floating toy start moving is a pulling force.

A toy boat starts moving when you apply a pulling force to it.

You can make a floating toy start moving by pulling it. This applies a pulling force to the toy. The toy starts moving across the **surface** of the water.

child's arm applies a pulling force to the toy boat

toy boat starts moving

Applying a pulling force will make a toy boat start moving across the surface of the water.

What Makes a Floating Toy Change Direction?

When forces act on a floating toy, they can make it change direction. One force that can make a floating toy change direction is a pushing force.

A pushing force can make a bodyboard change direction.

You can make a floating toy change direction by applying a pushing force to one side of the toy. The toy will turn in the direction of the push.

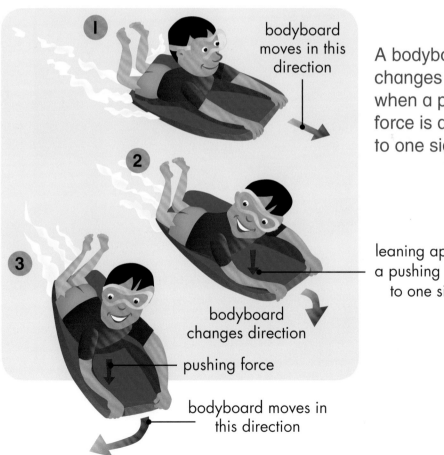

1 bodyboard moves in this direction

A bodyboard changes direction when a pushing force is applied to one side.

2

leaning applies a pushing force to one side

3

bodyboard changes direction

pushing force

bodyboard moves in this direction

What Makes a Floating Toy Speed Up?

When forces act on a floating toy, they can make it speed up. A pulling force that can make a floating toy speed up is **gravity**.

Gravity is a pulling force that acts on all objects, including this water and the rubber ducks.

When a river is on a slope, gravity pulls the water downward. The water flows faster, so the toy that is floating on it moves faster.

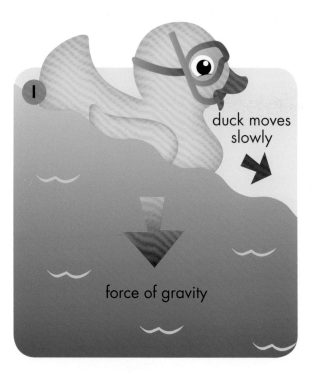

duck moves slowly

force of gravity

duck moves faster

2

force of gravity

duck moves even faster

3

force of gravity

The force of gravity makes the water and rubber duck speed up as they move down the slope.

What Makes a Floating Toy Slow Down?

When forces act on a floating toy, they can make it slow down. One force that can make a floating toy slow down is **water resistance**.

The force of water resistance is making this kayak slow down.

Water resistance is a force acting on objects moving through water. It slows things down. Water resistance pushes against the front of a floating toy and makes it slow down.

1 fast   kayak moves this way
force of water resistance

2 slow
force of water resistance

The force of water resistance on the front of the kayak slows the kayak down.

3 slower
force of water resistance

What Makes a Floating Toy Stop Moving?

When forces act on a floating toy, they can make it stop moving. One force that can make a floating toy stop moving is an **impact force**.

When this pool toy hits the side of the pool, it will receive an impact force.

When a floating toy hits an object, the object applies an impact force. If the impact force is large enough, it can make the toy stop moving.

1

direction pool toy is moving

2

impact force

pool toy stops moving

The side of the pool applies an impact force to the pool toy, making it stop.

What Else Affects How a Floating Toy Moves?

Another thing that affects how a floating toy moves is its shape. Toys of different shapes create different amounts of water resistance. This changes the way a toy moves.

A floating toy's shape affects the way it moves.

A floating toy that creates more water resistance needs a larger force to change the way it moves. Wide shapes create more water resistance than narrow shapes.

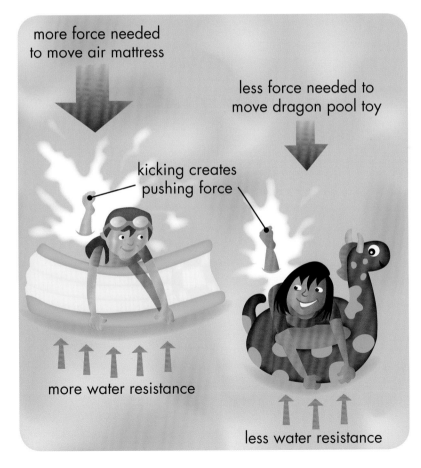

more force needed to move air mattress

less force needed to move dragon pool toy

kicking creates pushing force

more water resistance

less water resistance

More force is needed to move the air mattress because it creates more water resistance than the dragon pool toy.

Make a Floating Toy: Rubber Band-powered Boat

This rubber band-powered boat is quick to make and great fun to play with.

What you need:

- clean plastic meat tray
- pen
- scissors
- piece of thin, stiff plastic, such as plastic packaging
- hole puncher
- rubber band
- 2 matchsticks, heads removed
- bath or sink filled with water

Ask a parent or teacher for help.

An unwinding rubber band turns a paddle, which pushes the boat through the water.

What to do:

1 Draw the shape of the boat on the meat tray.

2 Cut out the boat.

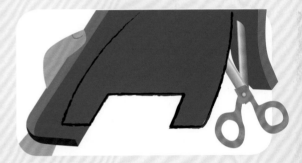

3 Cut a rectangular paddle out of thin, stiff plastic. The paddle must fit inside the cut-out shape in the back of the boat. Make it as large as possible.

4 Use the hole puncher to make two holes in the paddle.

5 Thread the rubber band through the holes in the paddle.

6 Hook the rubber band and paddle to the back of the boat as shown in the picture. Place the matchsticks on the outside edges of the boat to help hold the rubber band in place.

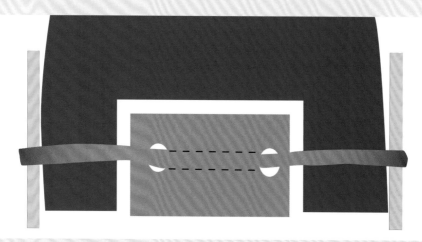

7 Turn the paddle backwards until the rubber band is wound up. Hold the paddle tightly to stop the rubber band from unwinding.

8 Still holding the paddle, put the boat in water.

9 Let go of the paddle. The paddle will unwind and the boat will move.

Experiment: Do Eggs Float?

Try this experiment to find out whether eggs float in different liquids.

What you need:
- measuring jug
- ½ gallon (2 liters) of cold water
- two waterproof containers
- table salt
- tablespoon
- wooden spoon
- raw egg (must be fresh)

What to do:

1 Use the measuring jug to pour ¼ gallon (1 liter) of cold water into each container.

2 Put six level tablespoons of salt into one container. Stir until the salt is completely mixed into the water.

3 Place the egg in the freshwater. Does it float or sink?

freshwater

saltwater

4 Place the egg in the saltwater. Does it float or sink?

What happens?

The egg floats in the saltwater but not in the freshwater.

The freshwater pushes up against the egg, but the pushing force is not big enough to support the egg's weight. The egg sinks.

If the egg floats in the freshwater, it means the egg is bad!

When you add salt to water, the water becomes heavier. The heavier saltwater pushes up against the egg with more force. The pushing force is big enough to support the egg's weight. The egg floats.

Something else to try

What happens when you float an egg in saltwater and freshwater at the same time?

1 Fill a container halfway with saltwater.

2 Very slowly pour freshwater on top, to fill the container.

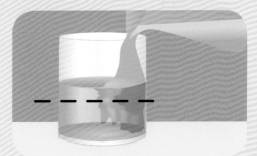

3 Wait a few minutes then gently place the egg in the middle of the water.

What happens?

The egg floats in the middle of the water. Saltwater is heavier than freshwater, so it stays at the bottom of the container. The egg floats on top of the saltwater.

How Forces Make Floating Toys Work

This table shows some of the pushing and pulling forces that act on floating toys.

Forces make toys . . .	Pushing or pulling force?	Example of the force acting on a toy	
start moving	pulling force	A toy boat starts moving when you apply a pulling force to it.	
change direction	pushing force	A bodyboard changes direction when you apply a pushing force to one side of it.	
speed up	pulling force	A rubber duck speeds up when floating down a slope because the pulling force of gravity is acting on it.	
slow down	pushing force	A kayak slows down when the pushing force of water resistance acts on its front.	
stop moving	pushing force	A pool toy stops when an impact force acts on it.	

Glossary

floating   resting on or just below the water's surface without sinking to the bottom

freshwater   clean, unsalted water, such as water straight from the faucet

gravity   the force that pulls objects towards Earth, and acts on everything, all the time

impact force   a force that acts on a moving object when it hits something

sinking   falling down through a liquid, such as water

surface   the outside or top layer of something

water resistance   a force that acts on an object as it moves through water and slows it down

Index